ACE

GUIDE DOG DETECTIVE

by

D.K. Adams

outskirtspress
DENVER, COLORADO

Dedication

Ace and I have shared this last year, our first, together.

I can't begin to describe what a large part of my life he has become, nor can I imagine my life without him playing his part in it.

As I mentioned in this book, his primary goal is to outlive me, something I remind him of daily.

As we continue our journey together I can't help but think of those who allowed us this special opportunity.

First of all none of this would have been possible without the extraordinary generosity of the people of our great country, The Veterans Administration, The American Legion Post 273, Southeastern Guide Dogs and the selfless dedication and training of Scott Lieser, his wife Emily, daughter Emma Grace and son Harrison who molded the first year and a half of Ace's life into the exceptional being he is today.

Also to the Kids and staff at Braden River Elementary School who raised $5,000.00 for the privilege of giving Ace his name. Ace is the ninth Guide Dog those Children have raised money to name. What a wonderful lesson they are learning in good citizenship. And how can I ever thank Alice Ryskamp enough who introduced me to Ace and trained us how to communicate.

This is the first book in a planned series chronicling Ace and my life based on things that really happen as we travel down life's road together. We both hope to see you again soon with our next adventure.

Ace & Ken ☺

Contents

A Special Acknowledgement

I would like to take this opportunity to give special thanks to a fellow veteran and my friend for over 60 years, Rich Holland.

Without Rich's tireless help and support this project would never have reached completion.

Thank you Rich, Ace and I are forever in your debt.

Ace Foreword

From the first moment I laid eyes, or in my case an eye, on Ace, I knew he was the one.

I can't put my finger on it but it just felt right. I soon realized that others might benefit from our experiences together.

Those who are in need of a guide dog, others who were approaching the need for one and also in helping the public in general realize just how wonderfully special these beings are and what a dramatic change they make to the quality of life to their owners.

This book chronicles the first year of Ace and my life together and the things we experienced while going down life's road with a humorous/tongue-in-cheek approach to the events we encounter.

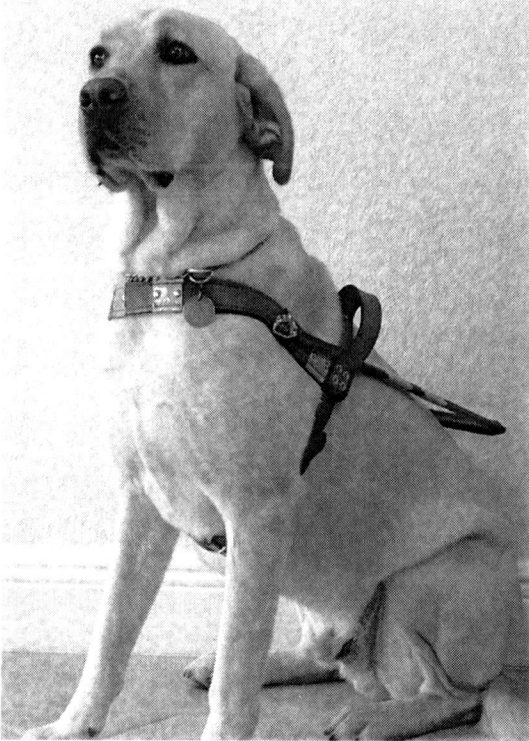

Ace Sitting

Chapter 1
Guide Dog Detective

I first met Ken the day he arrived at my school. My school is the Southeastern Guide Dog School in Palmetto, Florida.

Ken wouldn't have been my first choice as a roomy but that wasn't my call. He arrived late on the second day

Ace being chased off bed

of training and for a minute there I thought I didn't get picked or I didn't pass muster.

Little did I know that they already had me slated for this guy but were holding me back for his late arrival.

Oh, he was nice enough alright, but when you consider you may be spending ten years or so in the service of this person you hope the powers to be gave it the kind of in-depth vetting a decision this serious deserved.

But here we are and I for one am going to give it my very best shot.

I had only been in our room about ten minutes when he gave me heck for jumping on the bed.

I remember thinking; for cripes sake, I hope he is not going to be one of those fastidious tight butts I had heard the others talking about.

After all, I am a professional. I have been training for this position my whole life, surely he can cut me a little slack or this is going to be a long, long tedious relationship.

The rest of that first night was uneventful and I was eager to start the next morning anew.

As we got ready, and headed for the chow hall, it was apparent this guy didn't know his left from his right.

Would I have to start from square one with this guy? Surely he has learned something by this time in his life.

I'm sorry, here we are on the second page and I haven't introduced myself yet.

My name is Ace and I am a guide dog, more accurately a "Guide Dog Detective".

My new master, Ken, doesn't know that yet but he will just as soon as I get him trained.

This detective thing just sort of happened.

I was one in a litter of ten and it all started when we all would just be hanging out as pups do and I could always tell which one of my brothers or sisters cut the cheese.

I never missed. It was just a knack I had. It just grew from there and the next thing I knew, figuring out solutions to what others thought were mysteries, was just common sense to me.

It was as plain as the nose on your face or as we say the tail on your bum.

We Labs use the tail thing a lot.

Oh. not your Boxers or Spaniel types with those little teeny weenie stumps they try to pass off as tails.

They get a little sensitive about that, but the rest of us use the tail thing all the time.

Labs especially, are very proud of our mighty tails and if you have ever been swatted with one, you know what I'm talking about.

The problem I soon found was not being able to communicate to the talking class, what I knew.

Just being able to get through to someone with thumbs that could really do something with my information was next to imposable.

I had a serious talk with GOD awhile back.

She's a real neat lady.

What? You didn't know God was a female?

Don't you humans know anything for cripes sake? Didn't that "**Mother Nature**" thing give you a clue?

No wonder you need us.

Anyway, I ask HER, would it have spoiled some grandiose plan to give us thumbs?

Ace at five weeks old

SHE said yes, end of discussion.

Ok then, but I could have sure given up this sniffing everyone's back side just to get their pedigree. Couldn't we have swapped something out here?

Like I said SHE is real nice but don't ask HER to change something she is already committed to.

Anyway, I can handle this "not being able to talk" deal but thumbs would have been a real game changer. However, we have what we have.

Back to the task at hand;

I have been in training since I was five weeks old.

This shot was taken the day I started my training.

I will be two in January and here it is October.

Oh, I have had my problems all right. I've had three surgeries for one thing, or rather three things I guess, but only two were my fault.

The other had something to do with reproduction, whatever that is.

The other two were when I was young and I was experimenting as pups will do.

If I had thumbs things would have been different, at least for one of them.

You see, I ate a sock, OK, a silly sock, yes I know.

They gave it to me to play with and, well I got carried away and swallowed the darn thing.

Apparently it got stuck somewhere and they had to operate.

No big deal, am I right? Of course I'm right.

Next they had this ten or eleven foot piece of rope that I was playing with, well I was hungry. Labs are always hungry and I thought I would just see how it would taste. Just a little taste for crying out loud.

So I swallowed a bit of it and it was lousy.

But I didn't have thumbs so I couldn't pull the darn thing back out.

The only thing I could do was keep eating it till it was all gone.

Who knew that skinny little rope would get stuck too?

I don't know why they gave it to me in the first place. Didn't they know I would at least try and eat it?

Anyway, I do have two strikes against me and Ken might just decide to throw my butt under the bus because I am considered "Damaged Goods" for cripes sake.

What about this butt head they are assigning me to, he's not virgin material for cripes sake, you can bet on that.

Uh oh, here they come to take Ken and me to see the Vet. This could be trouble.

I pegged this Vet for a trouble maker from the very first.

There they go, telling him about all my surgeries, cripes sake, this Ken guy might just bolt for the door.

I'm really not all that bad and I think he has possibilities, but we may never get a chance to find out.

Maybe, if I look real sad, yeah, that's it, sad is one of my best looks.

Hey Ken, look, look, I'm sad, so sad see?

Ken is smiling at the Vet as the Vet says,

"You can turn this Lab back and make another pick, we have to make a complete disclosure about Ace's problems".

Here we go, Ken is about to answer the Vet, I'm holding my breath here. Who knows what this tight butt is going to say.

Well Doc. I have had over 40 surgeries myself so far and we were both born in January, Capricorns have to stick together, so as far as I'm concerned, this is a match made in heaven, I'll keep this one. He fits all my needs just fine.

He likes me! The son of a gun likes me! Well who would have guessed that. I'll be darned I have a real partner.

Now that's exciting, this is someone I can really bond with, I owe this one large.

OK, so he doesn't know his right from his left, I can live with that, after all no one's perfect.

I have to train him real hard, I want to be proud of him, show him off to the others. I have got to make him better than the boobs they got paired up with.

I only have 28 more days to get the job done.

But that's 28 days, full days, 24/7 and that equates to at least twice the time, and darn it I can make it happen, this thing can work.

Well for the next 28 days I pushed Ken real hard. I would get his sorry butt up at 5 AM, to go do my duty, then work him hard, real hard till 7 or 8 at night. I was making a real guide dog pilot out of this plow boy.

I remember one day at the mall. I almost blew it on that darn escalator. **"Escalator"**, escalator, I had a hard time with that command. Out of the 40 plus commands they drilled into my cranium that was the one I had a problem with.

Anyway, we are at this mall, a real big one. It spread out all over the place. Just keeping it all straight alone was a problem.

So, I was doing great, we started out at the food court and he gave me the **"Down Under"** command and I nailed it. I looked up at him.

Pretty good, don't you think? Ken, don't you think?

Yeah, he liked it.

Next they were going to move around the mall so he calls me out from under the table and gives me my next command **"Forward"**. Now that is one of my favorite cause we're moving baby. There are seven different commands that use the word forward, which means we are moving. I love going places.

Now I get the **"Left"** command so I move to the left

and follow along the wall.

No more commands so I just keep pulling Ken along the outer wall of the mall, passing all those stores, having fun and waiting for my next command but also watching for possible problems in front of us.

As a "Guide Dog" you have an awesome responsibility. You're always looking out for your master because he can't always look out for him or herself.

In turn, you receive unconditional love and that is what we "Guide Dogs" bring to the relationship to start with. It's more than just a job, it's a calling, and it's our life.

Back to my man and my next command to **"Find The Door In"** and into Macy's we go. Then the trainer tells Ken to give me another command to **"Find The Escalator"** I didn't have to look far cause there it was, just a few yards in front of us.

As we approach I get my next command **"Forward Up"** as we get on, Ken grabs my harness and gives me a hand up to make sure I didn't have a problem getting on.

I was doing alright but then I panicked, I know I couldn't believe it myself, I jumped straight up in the air, did a 180 and landed facing south.

Not good, I don't know what happened to me, I just freaked out.

A couple seconds later, I found my composure, my professionalism, and turned back north.

Boy was I embarrassed. I could get kicked out of the program for a goof up like that.

Here I am worrying about Ken, doing everything I knew to get him through the program so we could be lifelong buds and I screw up.

How will I ever be able to hold my head up again?

I felt just terrible.

We get to the top and as he is gently helping me, he says **"Forward" "Off"** followed with another **"Find the Escalator"** and I'm going to give it my best shot, looking as hard as I can for another escalator, and there it was about fifty feet on the right.

I pulled him on over to that escalator and get my next command **"Forward Down",** again he helps me by grabbing my harness.

Down we go, no panic this time, I was over it but the trainer wasn't quite as sure as I was so we did the whole thing over and over again until she felt sure I wasn't going to freak out again.

After that ordeal I get my next command **"Find the Door Out"** I can do this baby, I'm back on solid ground.

As I said, this is a really big mall and as we leave Macy's I hear Ken say to the trainer "I'm not sure which way to go to get back to the food court".

The trainer says to Ken "Just tell Ace to take you back to your chair"

Really?

Yeah.

So Ken does as she suggested and I jump into action and pulled him all the way around that mall right back to his seat.

I could tell he was impressed, I think I saw a tear in his eye. He loves me already, the big lug.

That was not a formal command but I knew what was expected of me and I rose to the occasion for my guy.

Back in our room that night I thought I might get heck for freaking out but he just grabbed me and hugged me like always, he still loves me.

The next week or so was filled with more long days and hard work as we continued to bond. Soon we would be finishing our last week. Gosh the time just flew by.

Well we made it, twenty eight days of sweat, re-dos, tired muscles, traffic, shopping malls, logging a lot of miles, and it is all coming down to this moment.

We made it this far but now it's the big one.

He has to pass the night test and that test comes the night before graduation or God forbid, non-graduation.

A simple pass or fail to them, but a life commitment or back to the drawing board to me.

God I hope he doesn't screw up, my toes are crossed and my tail wagging. With a little luck, just a little, oh please God, he's just a plow boy but he's my plow boy.

It is pitch black out, not a star in the sky and the moon

isn't giving us any help either.

He has to let me guide him around the grounds without second guessing my moves.

Can he do it, will he do it?

Well it's our turn, it's sink or swim baby.

We're off, no turning back now, this is the real Magilla.

Well, we are into the first turn and I can tell he's a little tense but doing OK, yes, keep it together baby, second turn good, third, still OK come on, come on you can do it big guy.

Down the back stretch, this is a little windy and it might make him think I am off the trail.

But no, he is going with it, the big lug.

OK, OK now around the far turn, now down the home stretch, come on baby, come on don't blow it now we are almost home, I can see the finish line and he did it, he didn't blow it. He did it just like I trained him.

God was I proud of him, my partner. Partner for life. Put that in your Funk & Wagnalls baby.

Chapter 2
On Our Own

The song "Me and My Shadow" comes to mind, just Ken and I doing our thing. We are on our way home.

Home, that has a nice ring to it.

This will be my permanent home. Not just one of those places to stay until I get to the next phase of my training or career, but my own home.

He has that Blonde with him, driving us, I'm good but I can't drive the darn car for him.

Here we are again where those thumbs would really have come in handy, are you listening God?

I hope it will be nice, I hope I will like it.

I am fraught with anticipation and questions like, will I be able to sleep in the same room with him and Blondie, like he and I have been doing this last month?

Will I have my own bed or just another piece of rug like I had back at school?

Oh well, whatever it is, I'll live with it as long as we are together.

Here we are, that's neat underneath parking, that's not bad for when it's raining, not that I mind the rain, living in Florida you got to love the rain.

Here we go, I'm liking this so far and he puts my harness back on, that was nice of him to take it off while we were traveling. Then I get my first command, I am working again, duty calls, **"Find the Elevator"**

An elevator, not a load of steps to climb, that's good.

"Forward off". Wooo we are pretty high up here. We must be six or seven floors up.

Would you look at this view, it's a shame he can't see it like I can, it's fantastic.

OK here we go inside, the anticipation is killing me.

After all, this is where I will be for the rest of my life, God willing.

Wow, would you look at this place, I think I died and went to heaven.

Ken, is this heaven? I feel like a king.

Oh, that's nice he is taking off my harness, I must be off duty now. I have got to check this place out.

But, first things first, where is the food?

Where is the feeding station, my bowl, where, where?

Ok, I see the bowl but its empty, what's with this empty bowl crap. I guess it's not time to eat yet.

These humans with their time for this and time for that, it drives me nuts.

I didn't see a slab of carpet anywhere. You don't think they are going to make me sleep outside on the balcony do you?

Ace and empty bowl

Don't get me wrong, I am, if nothing else, obedient and I will do whatever I am told. I have over 40 commands that they drilled into me during my very intense training, that I obey so I will stay where I am told to stay without question.

They think those 40 plus commands are all I have. I have at least a hundred more they don't even know about but let's just keep that between you and me.

What's this? More rooms, he is taking me down this hallway. Oh I get it, this is where he sleeps with the blond female, she must be his mate or something because she acts like she owns the place.

Yes, I see your **big** bed. You can bet your sweet butt I'm not going to be sleeping there.

What's this, this gorgeous piece of padded comfort lying beside his bed?

What is he showing it to me for?

Ace in his bed

He acts like he wants me to get in it, Ok, I'll play along. Here, I'm in.

I think he wants me to lie down, yes, yes there it is the command **"Down"**.

Surely this couldn't be my bed?

Is it, it is, is this a great guy or what?

I hit the mother lode baby, I wished those other guys in their double wide's could see me now.

What more could a dog, I mean a "Guide Dog Detective" asks for?

Maybe a crime case or two to be working on, but that's it, Oh, and food, lots and lots of food.

That's it, that is all, no kidding, but you got to include the food.

He gives me a little treat from time to time and he rarely yells at me so we are copasetic as far as I am concerned.

I can't wait to get involved with our first real case.

I wonder what it will be? Homicide, Burglary. Extortion, God, just talking about it makes my juices start flowing.

Oh, just look at me I am drooling all over the floor here.

Oh, oh there he goes. Ken the guru of the paper towels.

He is heading for the paper towels again.

Every time I drool he grabs the paper towels, I can't help it I just drool, get over it for cripes sake.

It is obvious that I am going to be the one that gets our professional life started here.

We could be having a crime wave all around us and he wouldn't see a dang thing. I know he is legally blind, that's why he has me but I have got to find a way to improve our communication skills.

Everywhere we go I am constantly looking for something we can make into a case.

We only need a couple that I can solve quickly and when the word gets out we will have more work than we could handle, I am sure of it. I will have to give him the credit of course but I don't mind living in the shadows. That's what "Guide Dog Detectives" do.

Chapter 3

The Raceathon

Ace, Ken, & Joyce rounding the first turn

Well here we go; they have my leash on and my harness in hand. I wonder where I will be working today.

We are going in that nice Lincoln Navigator so who cares? It will be a nice ride there and back if nothing else.

Here we are, this looks like a nice hotel, we can't be staying here though, they didn't bring any of those cases he seem to need, like the ones he had at the school.

Oh, we are going to eat, rather they are going to eat. That means I go under the table and make nice and don't beg, for gosh sake.

If I ate as much as these two do I wouldn't even fit in that Navigator.

Ok they're finally done eating, now here we go on outside, I wonder what's next?

I'm getting a whiff of dog, yes I definitely smell dog, I do, I smell a lot of dog, this could turn out to be alright if I get to meet another dog or two.

We are headed down closer to the water.

I can smell the water and the aroma is getting real strong but the aroma of dog is stronger still.

Holy crap! Look at all those dogs.

I didn't even know there were that many dogs.

What is this, a dogathon?

Big ones, small ones, there must be thousands.

Hey guys, what's going on?

Hey Golden what's happening?

Hi Lab, it's the big annual walkathon for "Guide Dogs".

Oh yeah, I heard about this back at the school.

Hey Shepard, so what's the deal here?

Well, they all get together and talk, they let us meet & greet, then they all line up and start walking.

Where do they go?

You're not going to believe this one. They end up back

here.

NO WAY?

Way baby. Yeah, makes no sense to me.

Why don't they just stay here, extend the talking for a bit, we would have some quality time with others and save all that energy.

I'll never know what makes humans tick.

You've got to admit, humans are strange beings.

Hey Lab, I think there might be something in it for you if you get back here first.

Is it food?

I don't know but it could be.

Food, that has a magical ring to it doesn't it.

Well if there is a chance for food at the end, this puppy will be crossing the finish line far, far ahead of any of these deadheads.

Ken, Ken, let's get this thing going here, they're lining up.

You're going to miss the food, I mean the start, let's get up close to the starting line.

Come on, come on, we can beat these ninnies.

As I was pulling him toward the starting line I looked back.

I had not noticed but he put on a T-shirt, one from the school, so did she, and I have my matching scarf on. Boy, do they look good, do we look good, I am so proud to be part of this family.

God he can be hard headed.

I can pull and pull but he just won't let me pull him into a winning position in line and they are about to start this darn race.

Hey, Lab, this is not a race. I'm told it is something called a Walkathon or something.

If there is a possibility of food at the other end it's a race as far as I am concerned and I'm winning.

They're off, come on Ken get your butt in line.

Crap, we are at least a quarter of the way back in the pack and there is no way that I am not going to win this thing, period.

Come on Ken let's get it. I have got to hand it to his blond mate, she is a real trooper, I think she wants a win as much as I do.

We are through the starting gate, through the first turn and doing fine. We are winning if I have to pull his cotton picking arm off.

By the time we hit the second turn at the pier we had shot into the lead.

Come on Ken, I knew we could do it.

I have this need to win and now that we are in the lead, there is no turning back now, it's time for record setting.

I got this babe, you and me Ken, oh, ok you can include the blond but we are headed for pay dirt.

Would you look at that? The cops are still setting up the final barricades and we are pushing their butts.

GET A MOVE ON COPPER!

You know we could be in line to set a new record here.

I just looked back and I can't see any of those others. Could I have made a wrong turn?

Are we still on the course?

Darn it, I hope I didn't screw up after I have been ragging on Ken all morning.

Wait, there is a green staff shirted person up in front of us, we could still be OK.

We are, keep on truckin' Ken, we have got this thing in the bag baby.

One more turn and then a hundred yards to the finish with no one in sight behind us, hip, hip hurray.

As we made the last turn the green shirt person counts, "Seven, Eight" What the heck is she talking about.

Well thank God Ken is questioning her.

"Those people up there are in front of you".

NO WAY, they didn't run or walk the race, they must have just joined in but trust me they were NEVER in front of us.

You tell her Ken. You've got to love him, he is always there in a pinch.

Well she wasn't giving any ground and neither was my partner.

Come on Ace, kick it up a notch and let's smoke these line jumpers.

You got it boss, and we were off to take the lead from these poachers.

I kicked it in high and we were off. The blond did real

good, she had as much grit as the old man.

We soon smoked those people like there was no tomorrow, crossed the finish line at least twenty yards in front of the closest one of those intruders. YO!

I was so proud of winning, for me of course and for my partner. Those others will see what a great team we are and they will remember us later when we solve our first case.

Where is the fanfare?

What! NO applause?

NO smiling faces?

No trophy?

NO FOOD?

What gives here?

He got me a drink, he always thinks about me, and they each had a bottle of water.

I feel cheated.

As we finished our water, I hear these two guys talking.

"Well we had better start getting ready, the finishers will be coming in soon".

SOON, what are we chopped liver?

Crap we have been here for fifteen minutes, no wonder there was no fanfare, these idiots don't even know we were in the race.

I pulled my heart out for my guy, to win this thing but also to show all the other guys my guy was the top of the heap, king of the hill, A-number one, stop me for cripes sake, I'm sounding like O'l Blue Eyes.

Well we won, I know it, he knows it and you can bet your sweet tushie all the other guys will know it, I'll see to that.

Ken is hobbling around, I think he must have a blister or something.

So here we go back to that fancy hotel for lunch and then home with our victory intact. We go without any fanfare but the pride of knowing, WE WON!

I'll sure sleep well tonight.

Chapter 4

Our First Case

Ace, Ken at dumpster door

We won the race but we still don't have a case to solve.

Í will just have to keep looking for one.

There has to be an easy one I can jump on and get us started.

So I am looking, looking everywhere we go for the makings of a case.

Back and forth to the store, up and down the beach, over the bridge to the American Legion, even when he takes or rather I take him, at his request to the VA Hospital always with one eye on our surroundings, always alert, after all that is what a "Guide Dog Detective" does.

So far nothing, the big goose egg, zero, nada.

Then one night he takes me out for my evening constitutional and I go about doing my business, he does the pickup thing, because as you will remember SHE, in all HER divine wisdom didn't think I needed thumbs, anyway he heads for the roll up garage door that houses the dumpster and just as he starts to pull up the door, BAM, I see and nail a giant rat, just inside the door heading for that dumpster.

Crushed his rib cage with one fierce bite, dropped him and stepped back just like the professional I am.

That fat rat was DOA baby, all accomplished by yours truly, Ace your trusty "Guide Dog Detective".

Hey Ken, Ken, did you see me? Did you see that?

Am I great or what? I'm great, you can't deny me, great is what I am.

Why are we getting out of here?

Ken, call the cops, this is it baby, our first case.

We'll find out where he came from, backtrack and get the whole gang.

They are going to love us around here.

Oh yeah, I can see the headlines now "Ace, Rat Slayer" or maybe "Ace, Guide Dog by Day, Rat Slayer by Night".

Ace w/ eye patch & rat

Why are we getting on the elevator? Ken, you have a cell phone, use it.

I swear this guy wouldn't know an opportunity if it bit off his tail, like that rat almost did mine.

Where is he taking me now? Ok, now I see, we are headed for the President of the Association's condo.

Smart thinking Ken, and just when I thought he didn't know what to do.

He's talking to him, telling him our story.

Tell him how I nailed that sucker, come on tell him. Wow, he's impressed, I'm getting a little praise, a nice pat on the head.

It was nothing, really, I could do that all day long.

Did you hear that Ken?

He said why don't you turn Ace loose in the dumpster room and let him get 'em all.

That's a great idea, let's get back down there and get this thing done, let him call the cops, they can see me in action.

Ken, what do you mean NO, you don't want me to get hurt or perhaps bitten by one of those vermin.

I can take care of myself, didn't you just see me in action?

So, that's it? He's just going to put out poison and that's it.

Teaching this guy how to parlay an opportunity into a case is going to be much harder than I could have ever imagined.

I will never understand how humans got the upper hand.

I keep going back to that thumb thing.

It's got to be the thumbs.

Chapter 5
High in the Sky

Ace, Ken & Airplane

Well it's that day of the week again when he goes to The Lighthouse to attend computer school.

I love the guy, but it's not always a romp in the park to be with him all the time.

I have to get in a cab, on the floor, with my head stretched up on his lap, try to look comfortable and not complain.

Maybe I should give up this detective thing and go for acting. I manage to pull this crud off every week.

If that's not bad enough, then after we get there, I have to spend the rest of the day under his darn desk, while he pecks around on a keyboard.

Let all the fun begin. Although, something seems a bit different today.

He packed one of those bags and put it along with my bone shaped little rug in the Navigator before we got in the cab.

Oh well, the cab is here and we are off for a fun filled day. The others that go in the cab with us every time always talk nice to me and he always sings my praises so all in all it's not that bad.

I think it must be time for his lunch.

What's this, it looks like we are leaving school a bit early today.

Wow, we are getting in the Navigator not that cramped cab deal.

We're not heading home though, it looks like we are going on a trip. I knew it when I saw that bag he packed.

It appears that the blond is not going with us.

Alone on a trip with my guy, just the two of us, there I go again explaining things using song lyrics. I can't help myself, I'm just a hopeless romantic.

Would you look at all these people, where is everyone going?

It looks like we are going to be waiting here for awhile because he just gave me the **"DOWN UNDER"** command.

That's where I get down with my rump facing him and he helps push me back as I do a backward shuffle under his seat. He doesn't want me to get my tail or toes tramped on. He's sweet and does look out for me that way.

I do get to take a lot of good naps on my job but it looks like we're moving again.

What the heck is this? It looks like a big drain pipe, you know the kind they have under roads with water running through them.

But this one has seats, what's with the seats?

Looks like we are taking one, the first one of course. He does like to be first, just like the two of us in that raceathon or walkathon, whatever they called it the other week.

They're closing that door, I wonder what is....Holy Crap! What is going on here?

He doesn't seem concerned, I'll give him a lick or two, see if he is OK.

Yeah, he's OK so I have to be brave too, can't let him know I am really scared, scared senseless.

I felt this same way the first time they had me on one of those escalators.

I freaked out till they calmed me down.

Those things are hard to prepare for.

I'll never forget it because that was my first **"FORWARD UP"** command.

It was before I met Ken.

Well this thing seems to be settling down ok and I can get back to my little nappy poo.

Oh, nap over and here we go again, now we are getting off, was this some kind of carnival ride?

This looks different, not like when we got on, what the heck happened?

Another SUV, not as nice but not bad and they want me in the back, the back, I don't ride in the back but for him OK. I got the **"FORWARD UP"** command again.

Were stopping and I smell dog, yep that's dog alright, I would know that smell anywhere.

Look at him, he's just a big puppy.

Hi, I'm Ace, we can play just as soon as I get your vitals, sniff, sniff.

What the heck are you?

Toby & ACE

I'm a Labradoodle and they call me Toby.

Well Toby you got anything to tug or chew on?

Sure I got plenty, do you want to see?

Let's do it puppy, let's do it.

What is she doing with that red thing of his?

I'm thinking she put something to eat in it.

When she drops that thing I am all over it, this pup doesn't have a chance.

Got it and I was right there is food inside.

The food is not easy to get to. Maybe if I bite it real hard, there.

Dad, Ace just ate Toby's Kong.

Ace, give me that.

What? I was just going for the food. She put the food inside.

It is always the same, they give you something then don't understand when you do something with it. Just like the sock and rope. I'll never understand humans.

Oh, well, let's get that rope tugging thing going Toby my boy.

Darn, I thought I had energy. This pup has it to burn, he's wearing my young butt out.

Hold on Toby, let's take a break.

Can't take it, look, look, the old guy can't take it.

OLD, who are you calling old? I just turned two a couple months ago.

Well Ace, that makes you over twice my age, old guy, HA, HA.

I have to admit he is full of energy but I have strength and maturity and pulled his buns all over that big, big house.

Thank goodness it's time for bed, I need sleep, sleep not just a nap, I'm tired.

Gosh, we had a great time, he darn near wore me out but I think that was the most fun I have ever had.

I wonder if this is what they call a vacation?

If so, I am down with this vacations thing, yeah baby.

I met two other, more mature, dogs at Ken's son's place and we stayed there for the next three nights. They were great dogs to just hang with but they didn't have the kind of raw energy that Toby had.

One day we went over to Ken's brother's place and what do you think? Yeah, you guessed it another dog.

This Columbus place must be dog haven because it seems every house has at least one dog.

It is sure not like that where I live because, as I may have mentioned, besides that cat on the third floor I am the only animal in the building.

I sure hope Ken is having as much fun as I am because maybe we will come back this way again.

It looks like we are getting ready to head back to our house. Frankly I could use the rest.

I feel like I have been binge playing.

I am definitely going to sleep when we get back into that small thing that shakes a lot and gets us back home.

GOOD BY COLUMBUS, WE LOVE YOU.

We do love them, don't we Ken? Yeah, yeah we love them.

Chapter 6
A Little Off the Top

Ace Relaxing at home

Back home and I could sure use some rest.

Here we are again, its Thursday and time for computer school again. Back in the cab, back under the desk, back in the cab, and finally, finally home.

Well at least that's over for another week.

What's this, it appears he is taking me out for a walk. I like taking him places and I think he likes showing me off.

I know I like showing him off but I don't see many other dogs, in fact only Guide Dogs are allowed on the beach.

That's kind of special but I haven't seen one other dog on the beach.

Oh, it looks like we are going to that dog friendly restaurant, "The Brown Boxer" just down the street.

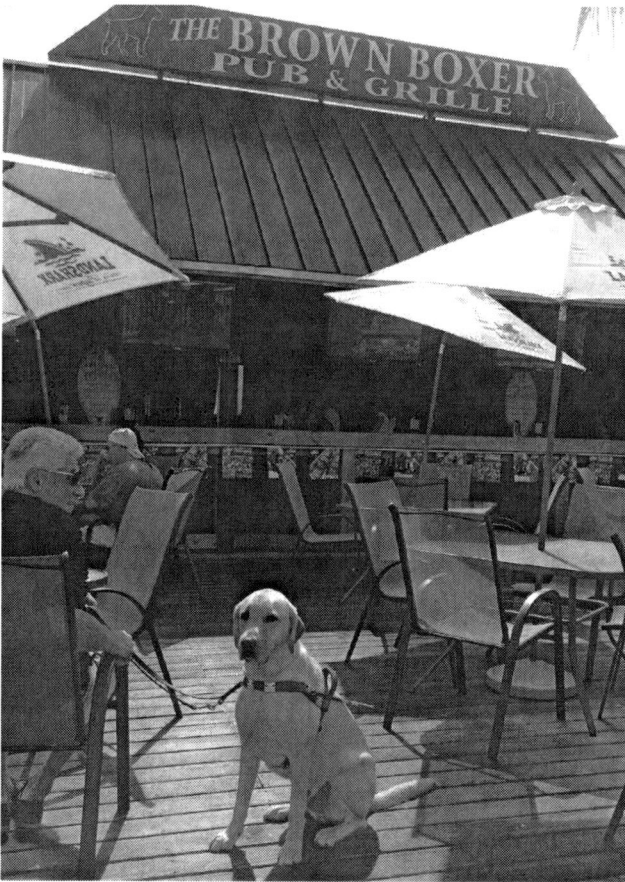

Ace at the Brown Boxer

I like it here, they bring me a bowl of water with ice no less, I just love chewing up ice cubes.

Oh, and a treat every time we visit, I get a treat.

It's just the opposite of the beach because there is always a good chance of meeting other dogs at The Brown Boxer.

Here come the waitresses, they love me.

They want to take my picture.

I'll have to give them my best look, no sad look for these gals.

Look at that, there is another dog at the next table, I hope he lets us get together.

Hey dog, what's happening?

"Not much, my master is here to try and raise money for my surgery".

What's wrong with you?

"I have this bone tumor and my guy doesn't have the money for the operation so they are having this fund raiser to help get the money".

I bet my guy will help, look he is talking to your guy now.

You know my guy is a DAV (Disabled American Veteran) and he knows about these things, I know he will get you some help.

Have you had surgery before?

Just once, I think, when I was real little, something about re-production.

Yeah, I know, I had that one too, but I had two others.

Did they hurt?

Na, I was a little sore for awhile but you get over it real fast, you'll see, you will be fine.

They are getting along just fine, exchanging stories, telling tales and look he is handing him some money. Did I tell you he would help, he's good that way.

Your guy's a Vet too, right?

No, he lost his legs in a car accident.

Oh, my guy thinks he is a Vet I can tell by the way he's talking. Look, they are talking about something in Iraq, he wasn't there but a friend sent him some stuff.

Now your guy just told him he's not a Vet.

That seemed to change the conversation somewhat. Well it looks like we are going, he wanted to get down here to meet your guy. Bye dog, good luck with your surgery.

Ken looks puzzled, I think he is going to talk to me even though I can't answer, he does share things.

I feel like Father Confessor some times and I'm not even Catholic.

Now he seems to be talking to his GOD, I'm going to need a score card to follow this thing much further.

I get it, he doesn't know why he had such a change in his feelings when he found out the other guy wasn't a Vet.

After all, he is still disabled, he still needed help. By making a nice donation, Ken still did a good thing but he made the mistake of assuming and we all know what happens when you assume.

I think he has a handle on it now, it was a good thing and he shouldn't feel bad about what he did.

The next morning we did our long walk on the beach. I could do that every day but it sure wears me out. Pulling him for over two miles is harder than it looks.

Ace in the grooming tub

Back home for a little while and we are off again, this time to that dog grooming place they call "Doug's Doggie

Stylz". They seem to like me there especially the owner Doug and I like them too but Ken has to leave me while they do their magic on me.

I like getting pampered, they do my toe nails.

What's this? A haircut, that will make me look good for my guy, Oh baby.

Ace on grooming table

Well they're done and I feel great. Here comes Ken to get me. He goes next door to a restaurant called the "Daiquiri Deck" to wait while Doug turns me into Mr. Wonderful.

Hi Ken, what do you think, am I handsome, am I, huh, am I?

He loves me, what's not to love and I love him, I guess he's my Mr. Wonderful.

Off to The Brown Boxer for lunch.

Hi Ace, Hi Ace.

The girls, they love me here, watch, here it comes, the bowl full of ice cubes, the treat, you got to love these girls.

Ace, what happened, did your daddy get you clipped? You got shaved didn't you, you sweetie you.

They like it, I knew they would like it.

This being a Guide Dog has a lot of facets to it.

It's not all that cut and dry.

Cut and dry, get it, I swear they just keep coming, I even surprise myself.

Chapter 7
Old Habits Die Hard

Ace eating rug

I know I told you about my troubled past, you know with the sock and rope deal, well it almost happened again.

Ken and I had been doing just fine together.

He and the blond took me to "The Club" they belong to. It's this real nice yacht and tennis club on Treasure Island and I'm the only dog allowed in the place.

Although there are a few other dogs on the boats around there, but in the Club I'm the only four-legged guest.

One of the few little perks of being a service animal or in my case, can I get a little drum roll here, "Guide Dog Detective."

We have been doing a couple miles on the beach several times a week or going over the bridge to

The American Legion, the grocery store, drug store and way up the road further to his friend's house.

His friend doesn't have a dog but he's nice and I think he likes me, but then again what's not to like?

Anyway, things were going just fine although I had missed a few commands because I was thinking about cats, squirrels and rats, really about those rats. You know if Ken would have just run with the rat thing we could have been working full time on detective work by now.

He just doesn't get it yet but I'm still working on him.

I know, I know, I am running this rat thing in the ground but you know what I mean.

Now all the rats are gone, I know because I check every night when he takes me out to do

"Busy, Busy". That's the command for doing your business, or potty stuff as you may call it.

We had a busy morning, (That's just one busy not **Busy, Busy)** out to the grocery, a long walk on the beach and then home for a nap.

Ken was relaxing on the sofa not paying any attention to me and I got hungry. I looked the whole place over, every nook and cranny for just a small scrap of food but nothing. Ken was still enjoying his little nappy poo.

I stretched out on the rug at his feet and took a little nap myself and as I lay there I started sniffing the rug I was lying on.

It smelled kind of different. I sniffed it for a while, I think I should know that smell, that aroma, then I took one of those little pieces of fringe-like things and bit it. It came off so I ate it. It wasn't half bad and the taste was kind of familiar but I couldn't put my paw on it.

I thought maybe if I eat another, the taste of what it was just might come to me.

Hide, by gosh, that was what the taste was, hide, it tasted just like hide. Not unlike those rawhide bones they occasionally give me to chew on.

I knew if I ate enough of it that taste would come to me,

I guessed it; it was rawhide.

I knew sooner or later with my detective instincts I would solve another mystery.

It took longer to figure out than I would have thought. I am normally really good with this kind of stuff.

Hold on just a minute, it couldn't have taken me that long to identify the rug as being made of rawhide, could it?

I think I could be in just a little bit of trouble here.

I just may have eaten more than I thought.

Dog gone it, surely I didn't eat that much.

My appetite gets the best of me sometimes and it looks like this just might be one of those times.

Boy, am I going to be in trouble.

If they have to perform surgery on me again, I'm a goner. Sure I might survive the operation but there is no way he will keep me then. I can't even cover that hole with my bowl and I can't lie on this spot for the rest of my life.

Oh, for cripes sake, he's waking up, now what?

Maybe if I just scoot over on top of this giant hole he won't even see it.

Yeah, that's what I'll do, I'm always thinking, that's why I'm such a great detective.

Gosh I'm good, he just walked out of the room and didn't see a thing.

Uh oh, I just moved and he's back,

BUSTED. DANG.

OH, he is REALLY MAD.

I really let him down.

What's wrong with me?

Here I'm thinking of how great I am while I hurt and let down the only one who really loves me, how am I ever going to get out of this one?

What if he just gives up on me and turns me back-in to the Guide Dog School?

What would I do then?

I could never find another guy like this one.

He grabbed me by the snout and is shaking his finger at me, telling me just how disappointed he is.

Gosh, I could just die, I didn't mean to disappoint him, I didn't realize what I was doing, you know. I knew I was eating but I didn't realize I was doing damage to his stuff. He has banned me from the den, I have to sit or lay outside the door.

I am giving him my very, very best sad look but it doesn't seem to be working.

I may have really done it this time. If I could just tell him I am so sorry, I didn't think, I love him; I'll try harder not to disappoint him again.

I have been outside that door for about an hour now. He probably called the Guide Dog School to come and get me.

What's this? I think he is calling me in. Yes he is, he is calling me into the den. He's petting me. He still loves me. I promise to do better, I really will.

If he only knew what I was saying or how I feel. Then again, the way he is looking at me, I think he really does.

Chapter 8
When You're Good, You're Good!

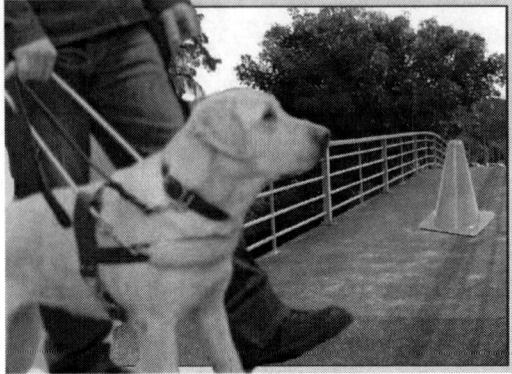

Trouble on bridge

As a Guide Dog you have to always be alert. Just yesterday we were over at The American Legion, he likes to go over a couple times a week for lunch and to chat with other Vets, so on the way back as we were crossing the draw bridge, they had an access panel open that took up most all of the walkway.

They had a little bright orange cone out but that was all and as I got close I realized that there was about a 30 to 40 foot drop straight down.

I bristled immediately, stuck out my right shoulder in his direction, stopped his forward movement, and then inched him slowly around the right side.

Boy was that close, he could have been killed or very seriously injured.

I have a very responsible job. When I put on my harness, I am all serious business, that's why I can't be petted when I'm working, it's not because I don't love kids because I love them all.

About a month later Ken had told one of the cabbies that takes us to and from the VA Hospital about our experience on the bridge.

A couple weeks after that, we happened to get that same cabbie and she stated that she got caught as the bridge opened one day so she got out of her cab and tore into those workers who had left that access panel open while they took lunch or a break the day Ken and I almost fell in.

But she didn't stop there. She had one of the bridge tenders in her cab a while later and gave him a piece of her mind about the same issue.

When Ken heard of her efforts he thanked her profusely and gave her a handsome tip.

We got back from the Legion around 2:30; I know because that is when I get my afternoon meal and as we all know Labs love food and will never willingly miss a meal.

Anyway I had just finished eating when the blond called from her work to say that she had just gotten a call saying that I, Ace, your Guide Dog Detective, did a poopoo in the elevator.

Thank goodness I am a detective at heart, this was just up my alley, a real case but in this case I was the number one suspect. I had to do my best work; my reputation was on the line here.

I have to hand it to my boy here, Ken always has my back, and he is really great that way.

Luckily we had two guys working on the storage closet just outside our front door, that's where they keep that large container with all that food I really love, but getting back to the case, and one of them had reported the "poopoo" accident in the elevator 20 minutes before we had returned from our outing to the Legion.

You see we live in a Condo that doesn't allow pets, I know, I know, people who have pets think that's ridiculous and I am sure you feel that way or most likely you wouldn't be reading this book, but there are places like that and people who live there have the right to restrict pets if the majority of the owners vote to do so.

However, in the case of service animals, of which I am one, the law says service animals can't be restricted from any place open to the public, which includes housing; that would be discrimination because he needs me to get around safely.

But there are still some owners who don't like the fact that I live here and are just looking for a reason to blame me for anything that goes wrong if they can. That is why I always try and be on my very best behavior.

All the more reason we have to either prove we didn't do this dastardly deed or if we had, claim responsibility and make some kind of retribution and apologize, because accidents do happen to all of us.

In this case we know we are innocent and this is where my detective instincts take over, he is so lucky to have me in times like this.

Now even though our worker reported the accident to a Lady in the lobby 20 minutes before we got home, she called the President of the Condo Association to complain about ME. ME, GUILTY?

Guilty without even a chance to explain or prove my innocence?

Now the president called the blond, not Ken and the President only lived three doors down the passageway.

Ken is pretty protective of me and I think that is why he didn't want to accuse him directly, which was probably the right course of action on his part.

When Ken got the news, he acted like a seasoned detective himself.

I was amazed, I knew there was a detective inside him somewhere, and there it was shining brightly.

Without going into the messy details, he developed a timeline, backed it up with the statements from the two workers, established that the droppings weren't from yours truly, wrapped it all up in a neat little bundle and dropped it in their laps.

Then Ken said, "Let's go to the video" because we have security cameras on the property, but not one of them wanted to or would, they didn't apologize they just said "Lets just forget it".

Case closed, God I love this guy.

He wasn't too happy because he wanted to use that video to rub it in their hair, that's just the way he is.

Chapter 9

Home Away from Home

VA Nursing Home

We spend a lot of time at the VA Hospital Complex just short of a mile from our place.

This year he and the blond decided to observe the Memorial Day services held at the cemetery on the grounds.

It is his intent to be buried there but he had not visited the cemetery before this service.

The important part was that there were dogs at the service. Oh there were lots of nice people but there were dogs. I love dogs, I love being around dogs, you know what I am talking about, like you feel about being around people.

Anyway, it was a great time and I saw several dogs and

we were getting ready to head out on our way home when we headed past this group of people standing around this guy who was talking.

Well I could see a little further than that and I charged forward. I know, I know, forgive me I was out of control. I charged forward between this guy's legs from behind, then through another, also from behind and there I was face to face with the most beautiful little, actually she was almost my size, little French number (Standard Poodle) who was the service animal of the Marine, in dress uniform, who was talking to the group I had just assaulted with a rear attack.

There I go again, but she was sooo beautiful I couldn't control myself.

Unfortunately she didn't share my enthusiasm for what I saw as a long lasting relationship so I retreated with my tail, proud as I am of my tail, tucked neatly military style between my legs and willing to take on the wrath of my owner for my unruly behavior.

Scold me if you will, I thought I might be in love.

He is a helpless romantic himself so he just gave me a couple of tugs on my leash and had me take the blond and him back to the car.

We came across a couple Vets in wheelchairs from the VA nursing home on the property and they were really nice guys and they seemed to like me.

Next I hear him talking to someone from the nursing home who said they would love a visit from me.

Me, can you believe that they actually want to see yours truly? I wonder if they need a detective, because if they do, I'm their guy.

We headed on home for the night but I could tell we would be back to see these Vets again real soon.

Well, I was right, it wasn't long till we were over at the VA nursing home to visit all those great Vets.

When we arrived at the VA nursing home we were greeted very warmly and were welcome to walk around and visit with Vets who showed an interest in our visit.

One of the first was a Vet in a wheelchair and well into his nineties. He appeared almost motionless with no expression on his face.

When I approached him, gave him a sniff and a wag of my mighty tail, you could see the change come over him.

He very slowly started moving his right arm toward me and patted me on the top of my head.

I licked his hand and his face lit up like a Christmas tree.

He then moved his left arm in my direction and held my head between his hands. He patted the top of my head again and again and just smiled.

We spent about ten minutes with this Vet who never uttered a sound but his huge smile was words enough for me and my guy.

We felt we brought a lot of good cheer with our visit that day but none more rewarding than that very first Vet.

This won't be our last visit I could tell that and one I hope we will make regularly.

Chapter 10
What's With That?

What's with the things people do?

As hard as I try, I just can't figure them out.

Let's go back a second. Remember the sock, the rope, and the rug I ate?

They knew that, God help us, Labs are always hungry, even you know that by now and yet it's like they always want to test us or something.

Give us an inch where food is concerned and you are creating a recipe for disaster.

People do other dumb things as well, things in other areas besides food.

Like just yesterday, he takes me to one of my favorite places, The Brown Boxer, a restaurant two blocks down the street.

They cater to people with dogs.

So we are sitting there having lunch, they always bring me a big bowl of ice as soon as they see me cause they know I love their ice, anyway, two people come in with dogs.

Well I get all excited, they both get excited, but do you think the people will let us visit and play a little?

NO, sit, stay, be good, down.

I just don't get it why they even have a place that caters to dogs if the dogs can't enjoy it.

It should be "A restaurant that caters to people who like to look at other people's dogs."

Now that would make sense.

And this kind of thing happens all the time.

I am a guide dog, I get that, but some of the restrictions just don't make any sense at all to me at times.

He was playing with me in the tennis court the other day. We go into the court, close the gate and he would throw the ball and I would humor him by getting it and bringing it back so he could throw it again.

I try to amuse him that way cause, let's face it, the man needs some exercise.

Anyway, we both have a little fun, but when the Guide Dog School people see it on one of their visits to check up on me they had a fit.

Apparently he is not allowed to play catch with me because they are afraid I will break ranks when we are out and about and I see a bouncing ball and drag his sorry butt out in front of a passing car or something.

I would never do that but some other guide dog might so all of us have to give up chasing, catching, and retrieving balls.

It's just doesn't seem fair.

But our job is keeping our masters safe and sound and

sometimes the rules are broader than we think necessary and yet overall the rules do work.

The same is true with a Frisbee.

He bought a bright colored Frisbee that he could see. He still has a little vision in his right eye and he wanted to play with me.

But here they come again. It seems that the same rules apply to Frisbees as tennis balls, NO.

No Frisbees, no tennis balls.

I guess it's a small sacrifice, but it sure was fun while it lasted.

Hey, if you don't have a dog, get one. If you have a dog be sure you play ball and Frisbee with him if you can. It's lots of fun for dogs and you may enjoy it as well.

Chapter 11
Up, Up and Away.

Well here we are again at that place I think they call an airport where we get in those little seats and visit dogs when we get out.

I sure hope I get to visit with Toby again.

This time it is really crowded and I have no room to lie down.

I can't sit here between his legs for several hours, well maybe I can if he needs me to but it sure won't be easy.

Luckily just an hour into our flight we land and change planes.

Now I have all the room I could ask for, this is great.

Well here we are, I have seen the guy who picked us up before, he has a dog, not a very friendly dog but a dog just the same.

He doesn't seem to have the dog with him; I think his dog's name was Cessna or something like that.

Back out of the car and I think I smell Toby, I do I smell Toby. I can't wait to see that guy.

Hey, Toby, how goes it bro?

Great Ace, how have you been?

Good Toby, real good.

Hey, hey Ace, they taught me some tricks since the last time I saw you, would you like to see? Would you Ace, huh, would you? I heard them say that you do lots and lots of tricks, would you like to see mine?

Toby my boy, settle down a bit, I just got here.

Fine, fine Ace, do you want to play tug with my new toy?

Yeah, just as soon as I get something to eat. Right now I need food, got anything in your bowl?

Nah, I ate it all buddy.

Ken, Ken, Ken, food, food, I need food.

He is getting better but he still needs plenty of work.

Here comes my food, see I told you he is getting better.

Ace, can we play tug now?

Sure, let's go.

OK but first let me show you my tricks.

OK, what have you got?

Well I crawl, like this.

Toby crawls across the floor toward Ace.

That's one Ace, by the way, how many tricks do you do Ace?

Well first, Toby my friend, in my case they are called commands, not tricks and there are over forty.

WOW, forty tricks, I mean commands, that's amazing.

OK, OK, here is my second. I roll over like this. Next my last and easiest I give them my paw like this. So what do you think? Did you have any trouble learning those?

Toby my boy, this may come as a shock babe, but of all my forty-one commands, none are crawl, roll over or give my paw.

Really?

Really Toby.

So I do three tricks that you, Mr. Wonder Dog, can't do.

It's more like won't, not can't my friend.

Ok, now let's tug, grab the other end of this thing Ace.

That pup Toby has more energy than I remember or maybe I am just tired from the trip but I am all tuckered out and he still wants to play on.

Toby, babe, I need a nap, really bad.

OK Ace but hurry cause we got a lot of playing to catch up on.

Whatever, I'm bushed.

When I wake up it is time for "Busy, Busy."

Ken is pretty good at knowing my bodily function schedule so he is right on top of it and we head outside.

This is different. He is letting me go without a leash. This is new territory and I like it.

As he walks with me around the back yard of Toby's house I spy a bicycle in the shrubs and immediately recognize this as a potential case for a "Guide Dog Detective."

You've got to admit it, the kid has a nose for such things.

I go over to the bike and keep smelling around to try and get him to notice it.

Bike in grass

Finally he comes over and I can see that glimmer in his eye that he may just get it, this is a case waiting to be uncovered.

I can see it all now, a home break-in, the attempted get away on a kid's bicycle, abandoning the bike when safely away from the crime area. I feel like I am in my element, the place I was destined to be.

Ken certainly can't blow this one; it's all right there in front of him, now just follow through big guy.

OK Ken, don't touch the bike; you know fingerprints and all the other evidence they might be able to find.

Now get in there and call the cops, let's get head and shoulders into this case.

Wow, at last a real case, I knew it was only a matter of time till I turned him around.

Here we go in the house.

He's asking about the bike. I guess that should be the first step, find out if they know anything, or recognize the bike.

The kid thinks it might belong to a friend of his

Well does it or doesn't it, this isn't rocket science here kiddo; a simple yes or no will work.

Press him Ken, don't let him off with "I think it could". Even if it does, that doesn't eliminate the potential for a crime scene here.

The kid's friend could be the perp.

It only makes sense that he then made the familiar getaway route toward his friend's house, then abandoned the bike and innocently walked on home.

Yeah, I think we have a scenario here to explain this abandon bike deal.

Now let's see how the kid reacts when questioned under a little pressure from the authorities.

I bet he crumbles like a wet suit.

His friend could have been perpetrating this crime without the kid ever knowing anything about a crime.

Also, he couldn't have taken very much and escaped on that bike.

If he didn't take much, the victim may not even know anything is missing yet.

It could have been just a little item or items.

This thing isn't over by a long shot.

I have got to keep Ken's focus on this case.

We have got to get our career as detectives off the ground.

At this rate I will be too old to sniff out clues by the time I get Ken trained.

Ah-ha, he admits the bike does belong to his friend.

But why is it just pushed into the shrubs? What about that?

The kickstand was not deployed, what about that?

LAZY, that's your answer, your friend is lazy!

They are all buying it. Do you believe this?

Call the cops and see if they had any break-ins in the area for cripes sake, what is wrong with you people?

You send them to school, buy them books and they still can't recognize their nose in front of their face.

I don't believe it.

Someone take my blood pressure for cripes sake, on second thought never mind I must be off the chart.

Toby, buddy, get over here with that tug toy of yours, I need to do some exercises before I explode.

Yeah, that's it, tug, tug, tug I need to expend some of this pent up frustration. That's the way Toby, tug, tug, OK, OK Toby I think that will do it. I have calmed down now. Let's rest a bit. Come on dog, rest for cripes sake.

Another missed opportunity.
Will this drought never end?
Enough already, Toby come on over here and relax a little bit. Stop tugging before I lose my mind. I'm reminded of "Watch what you wish for, it might just come true".

Toby and I had a great day tugging and the little sucker did wear my buns out, God that boy has a lot of energy.

Now I don't want to beat a dead horse but I am still waiting to hear that someone in this neighborhood has something missing to prove my point about the bike in the bushes.

I mean, how are we ever going to get a grip on crime if you won't even follow up on a lead that is handed to you on a silver platter?

The next morning we go to this big place they call a church and he takes me up front with a bunch of others and he gets a little food and drink. But does he think to share it with me? NO, hey, I could use a little something here. I am really not complaining, he gives me plenty but

I am always hungry, did I mention that before? Yes, I think I did.

Now we're off to another place, I hope there are dogs.

Hey, there is another dog, it's Champ, I saw him the last time we visited.

Hi Champ, how have you been?

Hi, Ace great seeing you again, I'm doing great, how about you?

Fine, just fine. Hey have you got any food you could share?

Yeah, I think there is something back in the kitchen, if you can get back there with all these people.

What's with all these people?

Oh the new kid they just got is having something at the church and then here.

I didn't see you at the church.

No, I stayed here; they don't take me there. But you, you lucky devil, you get to go everywhere don't you?

Yeah, it's good I guess, but I am always on duty when I am out of the house.

You mean you have to wear that leather thing all the time?

Yeah, unless I am in my house, then I can take it off.

I don't think I would like that. I used to think you had it great but I'm not so sure anymore.

How long it this thing going to last?

Beats me, it's my first.

We stayed a couple hours. Champ and I didn't get any playtime. In fact I didn't even get a chance to say good-by.

Well the bike deal is another missed opportunity because here we are again at that place that takes us home again and I am ready. Toby wore me out and I need some "ME" time to get over missing another chance to show off my detective skills.

Chapter 12
The Dog That Isn't There

It's nice to get home, I like to visit, but I miss my own space.

My own bed, bowl, and the place I like to go BUSY, BUSY.

I know it may not sound like much to you, but its pure heaven to me.

Here we are on chapter twelve and I feel I know you a little bit better. And let's face it you know a lot more about me. The life of a Guide Dog is a dedicated profession and it can get a little mundane for most of us but with this guy, well, he keeps it interesting.

If I didn't have my detective work and skills, I might add, I can see where it could get a little "Boring."

I am confident that there is a detective hiding inside this guy. It's a little deeper than I thought, but I'll get it to the surface, you can count on that.

Here's a news flash for you. He waited on a list for over a year to get me, right? He has had pets, and lived around animals his whole life and now after a year together he has developed an allergy to, of all things, Pet Dander. Pet Dander, of all the things for him to become allergic to, it's me, it's me.

But I'm not worried, he takes his meds every day and get this, I get a shampoo and a pedicure every week plus a clip every month. How is that for poetic justice?

The kid gets an allergy and I get the works, yeah, you got to love it. I mean I feel bad for him but I can't say that I got the crappy end of the stick this time.

I wanted to show you all of my forty plus commands and how they are used to help my guy but we haven't gotten through even half of them.

My problem is that I don't get to use them all the time either and I am always afraid that I may forget one of those seldom used ones just when he needs it the most.

I will share the one we use at the VA a lot and it always draws attention. It's actually two commands, first **"Right Around"** then **"Down Under"**.

We talked about this before, but it bears repeating.

He has had well over fifty appointments at the VA Hospital this last year so we have spent our fair share of time in those waiting rooms.

Anyway, he sits down then gives me the **"Right Around"** and I turn and put my backside toward him.

Then he gives me the **"Down Under"** and I scoot backwards under his chair.

I tell you it knocks them dead at the VA Hospital.

It kind of gives them a chance to see what I can do and one of the things I do is try to be inconspicuous, like

I do when he takes me out to a restaurant to eat and I disappear under the table.

Ace under the table

"The Dog that isn't there". That's me.

I have a couple more stories in me to share with you later and hopefully some good detective cases.

Chapter 13
Awkward

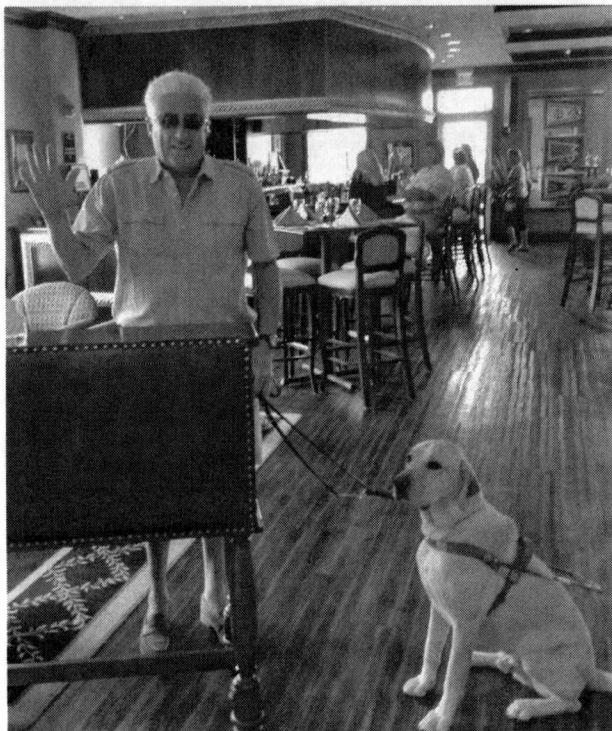

Me at the podium w / Ace at my side

Can I ask you to do me a big favor? Yes you, HELLO! Excuse me, thanks; I need a real big favor here.

Could you please move in real close, a little closer, yes, closer please, yeah, that's it.

That's good.

Thank you; I just don't want "him" to hear this.

From the first moment "HE" heard that I was writing

this book he has been bugging the crap out of me for some ink.

Ink, you know, verbiage, print, his "own chapter" in my book for gosh sake.

So after stalling, making excuses, conveniently forgetting, and anything else I could think of, I have painted myself into this corner and here we are.

Worst of all, I will have to give him an introduction, and trust me on this, "HE" will milk it like a prize Holstein cow.

He'll be milking long after the cow goes dry.

Don't get me wrong, he is a great person, but with an ego as big as—well you get the idea.

But here goes.

READERS, LADIES AND GENTLEMEN, MAY I HAVE YOUR ATTENTION PLEASE!

Thank you all for reading this and being wherever it is you are when you do read this, I hope you all are having a wonderful time.

I would like to take this opportunity to introduce my partner, my charge, my reason for being K----

What?

Give me a little more build up PLEASE for cripes sake. This is my paragraph, my big chance.

Yes, as I was saying, my reason for being in this business of guiding the visually challenged, and in my case, the mentally immature.

That wasn't a cheap shot; it's called levity, humor a little rib tickler. So get over it.

Gee-whiz.

Without further ado, here he is with his writing début, Mr. Ken Adams.

Thank you. Thanks to all our readers and especially to you Ace, for giving me this chance to show what I can do to perhaps help with the appeal for your little book.

Again, thank you the readers for making your way through the previous chapters of my friend's attempt at writing. Don't be too hard on him, he wears his emotions on his sleeve and will be blubbering all over these pages, giving us all, that trademark "Sad Look" of his.

Even when I know he is working me with that look, it tears my heart out; darn he is good.

Going against my instincts I will keep this short and hopefully sweet.

The few years before I met and was partnered up with Ace, I was having a harder and harder time getting around without injuring myself.

I kept tripping over things and falling.

I had surgery on one knee and both shoulders in addition to four concussions.

During this first year with Ace by my side, I haven't fallen once.

That in and of its self, is close to a miracle, and I owe it all to my best friend here, Ace.

Calling Ace my best friend seems so inadequate but I just can't think of a more appropriate term to explain just how important he is to the quality of my life.

Thank GOD for dogs like Ace and thank you for allowing us to share our story.

Thank you and please continue the story, guided by my best friend, Ace.

Wow, I for one certainly didn't expect that from my guy. Normally he's so into himself there is no place in the room for anything but him and his ego.

Dang, he put a lump in my throat; I think the boy really loves me.

God that's a great feeling, to know someone loves you as much as you love them.

It doesn't get any better than that.

Trust me, if and when you find it, protect it, nurture it and don't ever betray it.

You'll find it is the one thing that makes being here worthwhile.

What can I say, that's my guy and I'm his guide and that ain't all bad. ☺

Well here we are. It doesn't seem possible that it has been just over a year since I first met this guy.

It seems more like seven years but that's just my "Dog's Eye" view of things.

One year, wow, we have sure come a long way together, and I couldn't love him more.

I'd take a bullet for this one, and you know I think he might just do the same for me.

They say a Guide Dog has ten good years on the job and although I haven't made a detective out of him yet, this gig is far from over.

That would put him past eighty before I step down, and he told me the other day that my main goal was to outlive him.

I have to be honest, that's not my main goal, making this plowboy a bona fide detective is.

However I am a realist with only nine years left to go and frankly the boy is a little **s - l - o - w.**

This reminds me of a story I heard Ken tell as a little joke regarding drinking while we were at the American Legion the other week. It was about Sir Winston Churchill's famous responses when a member of Parliament made a derogatory statement about the Prime Minister's (PM's) drinking by peering out across the crowded chambers saying;

"If the alcohol consumed by the PM was in this chamber today it would reach a level about up to here", while making a jester with his hand indicating head high or eye level.

To which Churchill, took the podium, looked around the chamber, moved his eyes from head high ever so slowly up to the top of the very high ceiling and replied,

"So much work, and so little time," as the chamber erupted in hysteric laughter.

Like Churchill I have a lot of work to do in a short amount of time to complete the task.

So hang in there and I'll keep you posted, with another book or two, as we go through this thing together.

Hope to touch base with you in the near future. Enjoy!

Ace, Guide Dog Detective.

The End
of year one
☺

Guide Dog Commands
Obedience

Set, Down, Come, No, Stay, Heel, Stand

Do not use dog's name with these commands
Halt, Easy, No, Stay

Working Dog Commands

Forward, Forward in, Forward out, Forward up
Forward Down, Forward Straight, Forward Around,
Right Around, On, Off, Easy, Stand, Over Left, Left,
Left Left, Over Right, Right, Right Right, Follow,
Watch, Busy Busy

"Find The" Commands

FIND THE-
Curb, Door, Gate, Elevator, Escalator, Chair, Steps,
Aisle, Door in, Door out, Mailbox, Wall

CPSIA information can be obtained at www.ICGtesting.com
Printed in the USA
LVOW12s0826160514

385980LV00008B/160/P